SEARCHING QUESTIONS ON HEALING
A Christian Perspective

OWEN DOWLING

First in a Series of Studies
- Christian Perspectives on Healing -

ORDER OF ST LUKE

Searching Questions on Healing - a Christian Perspective

National Library of Australia
Cataloguing-in-Publication data

Dowling, Owen D. (Owen Douglas) 1934 -
Searching Questions on Healing - a Christian Perspective
ISBN 0-908460-30-9

First Edition 2005

Cover design and illustrations by Steven Hallam

Printed by Classic Press
18 Havelock Road, Bayswater VIC 3153

Published by The Order of St Luke the Physician in Australia
Unit 112, 100 Harold St
Wantirna Victoria 3152
Australia

Contents

SEARCHING QUESTIONS ON HEALING – a Christian Perspective

by Owen Dowling

General Introduction

This book is one of a series of study books on Christian healing produced by the Order of St Luke the Physician in Australia. Each book is designed to deepen the understanding and experience of healing. The suggested Bible readings, reflections and questions seek to stimulate thought and challenge the understanding of issues surrounding healing prayer and ministry. The series is suitable for either individual or group study and is relevant to experienced practitioners in the healing ministry as well as to those desiring to explore personal healing or wholeness in society. The Order of St Luke is both international and interdenominational and seeks to be a servant of the church and of individuals in relation to the healing ministry.

Other books planned in the series include:

The Search for Wholeness – a Christian Perspective.
Contemporary Models for the Healing Ministry.
'From Where I Stand' – Christian Perspectives on Healing.
Healing and Wholeness – some Biblical and Historical Perspectives.
Ingredients of Healing – a Christian Perspective.
The Contemporary Healing Smorgasbord – a Christian Perspective.

Information as to the publication and availability of books in this series is obtainable from Mrs. J. Coates, 112/100 Harold St. Wantirna Vic. 3152. Australia.

Preface

Owen Dowling has been involved in the healing ministry for many years. He has led many seminars, workshops, retreats and services on various healing themes. The questions raised in this book have come from the various avenues of learning, discussion and practice in the healing ministry in which Owen has been involved. They have been asked by different people at different times and give an insight into the issues which are significant for people seeking to understand and apply healing to their own lives and contemporary living. The book is designed either for private use or for use in a home Bible study / discussion / fellowship group. The readings, reflections and discussion questions provided are intended to stimulate thought, discussion, prayer and sharing rather than providing definitive or dogmatic answers.

Guidelines for Leaders of Group Studies

Each book in the series includes suggested Bible readings, the reflections and questions. These are intended to encourage a process of biblical reflection and group discussion. In healthy groups it is not essential for the leader to be the expert, but rather a fellow traveller in search of understanding. It is recommended that the discussion group have a leader who serves as a facilitator, helping group members to grow in understanding.

<u>Some skills and attitudes that will help leaders to be effective</u>:

The leader will:

- be a careful and attentive listener to other members' contributions, making sure that every member has an adequate opportunity to contribute to discussion.
- use questions to clarify contributions, stimulate discussion, overcome roadblocks and enquire after individual member's well-being.

- encourage the use of personal and honest language in the course of discussion. Authentic responses are ultimately more helpful than responses that only echo expected answers or provide religious clichés or generalities.
- strive for a good climate in the group, encouraging members to be at ease, and to be warm, friendly, encouraging and patient with one another.
- not be overly directive. Sometimes it is better to let a vital and exciting discussion run on than to cut it off prematurely just to make sure all discussion questions are covered.
- prepare the study, making sure that he or she understands the Bible texts which are suggested for reading and study by the group. Help from Bible commentaries or from the pastor might well be sought.
- encourage participants to read the study beforehand. If this has not occurred it may be wise to read through the suggested Bible passages in the group meeting. Questions like 'What stood out for you in the readings?' can assist discussion and sharing.

Helpful books for leaders

John Mallison, The Small Group leader. Openbook Publishers.
Greg Davies, The Model Small Group Leader Training Program. Openbook Publishers.

STUDY 1:

HOW SHOULD WE PRAY FOR HEALING?

Begin by reading ....

1. Psalm 30, especially verses 2 and 10
2. Luke 11:1-13
3. Mark 11:23-25
4. James 1:6,7 & 4:3

Some reflections ....

1. Both in the Hebrew Scriptures and in Jesus' teaching there are strong statements that God cares about us and that we can ask God directly and simply for help and healing. One of the mysteries of faith is that we can engage in this asking prayer.

2. Most of us waver in our faith from time to time. Many have an idea of God as the God of the universe but have difficulty conceiving that this God could be interested in the details of our need. Yet Jesus spoke about even the hairs of our head being numbered – a striking way of expressing his faith in God and his particular care for us.

3. Luke's version of the Lord's prayer and the following teaching, in its very simplicity and directness, challenges us to ask God for what we need, and to keep asking, trusting that God will give us what is good for us rather than what is harmful. However we note that Jesus taught that the requests were to be made along with and within the larger request for God's kingdom to come. This implies that our request should be in tune with that overarching one. James, in his blunt way, reminds us that we can ask wrongly, if we ask selfishly.

4. The style of praying that Jesus taught includes loving and worshipping his Father, having a trust in God which is expressed daily, and making sure that there is no barrier of unforgiveness as we pray. Luke's version of the Lord's Prayer makes this very plain indeed. 'For we forgive ....' suggests that we have actually done it. We often need help in coming to a point of forgiveness. When we cannot, we can ask for the power of the Holy Spirit to do so. To be able to forgive and to let go our resentments and desires for revenge is a healing in itself.

5. Should we pray for physical healing? We may have so spiritualized God that we think that God is only interested in the salvation of our souls. This seems to be contradicted by Jesus' teaching and practice. He told us to depend on God for our daily physical needs. He healed people of their physical ailments, restoring their bodies as well as their souls. We believe in the God of all creation, the creator of every cell in our bodies. Surely then we can ask God to order every cell aright when things have got into disorder. We are all confronted with the reality of dying and the wearing out of our physical bodies. No one can avoid this. St Paul speaks of our outer nature wasting away and our inner nature being renewed (2 Corinthians 4:16). So an appropriate time comes when it would be right to cease praying for physical healing, and to pray for whatever healing is needed in mind and spirit, and the restoration and healing of relationships.

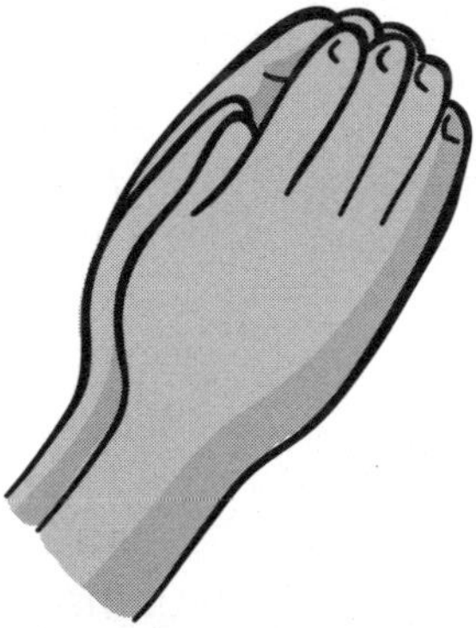

For thought and discussion ….

1. Recall times when particular needs have been met after prayer for help.
2. How would you describe ‘the prayer of faith’ which James’ letter mentions in connection with healing?
3. What are the important components of prayer for healing?
4. Write down a brief prayer for healing for a person (a mythical person whom you name). Share your prayer with the group and any insights you gain from other’s prayers.
5. Pray for, and lay hands gently on, any member of the group who requests it.

STUDY 2:

WHY DOESN'T GOD ALWAYS HEAL WHEN WE ASK?

Begin by reading ....

1. Genesis 4:1-7
2. Job 31:2-40
3. Mark 9:14-29
4. 2 Corinthians 12:7b-10

Some reflections ....

1. Early in the Bible we are confronted by the thought that God may accept the prayer and worship of one, and not of another. God reveals to Cain that his offering was not accepted because sin was 'crouching at the door' of his life and that he should beware lest it consume him. Cain is quite unable to hear and receive this, and shows that God's insight was right. He rose up in jealous anger and killed his brother. We realize that our heart may not be clean when we pray; we should examine our motives and our relationships. James in his Letter speaks of asking wrongly in prayer (see James 4:1-3), while Jesus, in his teaching, stresses the importance of forgiveness and forgivingness when we come to offer our worship. 'First be reconciled to your brother or sister, and then come and offer your gift.' (Matthew 5:24).

2. Job is a famous biblical character who protests his innocence before God, and his inability to understand why sickness and tragedy have come upon him. The long poem about Job challenges the traditional understanding, still common in today's world, that there must be an explanation for sickness or unanswered prayer for healing. The explanation must be that the person or their forebears have sinned. The Book of Job contradicts this, and so does Jesus. There will always be a mystery surrounding

the question of continuing sickness and seemingly unanswered prayer. Later Job says 'I have uttered what I did not understand, things too wonderful for me, which I did not know.' We should be wary of oppressing people with simplistic explanations, especially of the blaming kind, when they are sick. This is what Job's 'friends' did; it only made his suffering worse.

3. There are a number of occasions recorded in the gospels, where Jesus was distressed by the lack of faith on the part of his disciples. In Mark's account of the healing of the boy who had epilepsy, Jesus is exasperated with the people of his own generation and time: 'O unbelieving generation, how long shall I stay with you? How long shall I put up with you?' In private discussion with the disciples after the deliverance and healing as to why they couldn't accomplish it themselves he said 'This kind can come out only by prayer.'

   Clearly there was a depth of prayer behind Jesus' life and ministry enabling him to draw on the power of God more readily than most of us do.

4. There are various explanations given as to what was 'the thorn in the flesh' which Paul asked God to remove from him. One ready explanation is that it was a sickness or physical affliction of some kind. Canon Jim Glennon in his book 'Your Healing Is Within You' disputes this, giving evidence that the thorn in the flesh may well have been a troublesome person. In any case, there is the problem of unanswered prayer for even a firm believer. Three times Paul pleaded with the Lord to take 'the thorn' away from him, but God said to him 'My grace is sufficient for you, for my power is made perfect in weakness.' Many a Christian has found strength in those words to sustain them in difficult times. The quick removal of any problem after prayer may lead to lack of a mature and tested faith. Jesus spoke of persevering in prayer and lack of ready answers. In the

healing ministry we often encounter gradual healing. We also encounter situations in life where there is no physical healing, but other kinds of healing take place – healing of attitudes or relationships. Trusting God in the midst of our darkness and seeming lack of clear-cut 'answers' may be an important part of our faith journey.

For thought and discussion ....

1. How have you (and other members of the group) dealt with 'unanswered' prayer?
2. What are some of the blockages or barriers that can occur as we pray for healing?
3. Share instances where you or another person have been oppressed by supposed lack of faith and condemned by today's 'Job's comforters'.
4. How can we help those who have been bruised or oppressed by wrong or simplistic answers to their dilemmas and apparent lack of healing?
5. Consider the best way to minister to those with seemingly permanent disabilities.

STUDY 3

WHAT IS THE DIFFERENCE BETWEEN HUMILITY AND A POOR SELF IMAGE?

Begin by reading ....

1. Matthew 5:3,5,8
2. John 8:35,36 and 14:16,17
3. Romans 8:15-17
4. 1 Corinthians 6:19,20

Some reflections ....

1. At first sight, this question doesn't seem to be directly related to the healing ministry. Yet it could be that because of a poor self image, or because we feel we are not worthy to have God's attention, we may refrain from directly asking God for healing blessings for others, and most especially for ourselves. There is a kind of humility, parodied by Charles Dickens in his character Uriah Heep, which is quite unhealthy. He is ever so 'umble'. It can actually be a form of inverted pride which may disguise some angry and negative attitudes. The meekness described by Jesus as one of the characteristics of those who would be followers of him and inheritors of his kingdom, is often thought of as a sign of weakness – 'meek as a mouse'. True humility and meekness however is a strength. We choose to be humble and respect others. We withhold our own self-assertiveness quite deliberately. Paul speaks of drawing on the meekness and gentleness of Christ to teach him, and us, when to be humble and when to be bold.
(See 2 Corinthians 10:1 & 2)

2. One of the basic understandings of Jesus' teaching and the New Testament writers is that we have a standing as sons and daughters of God which can give us a sense of

freedom and boldness in our relationship with God and others. According to John, Jesus spoke of our membership with him in God's family as being sons and daughters rather than slaves. Exactly the same thought is taken up by Paul in Romans 8 – 'you did not receive a spirit of slavery falling back into fear, but you have received a spirit of adoption whereby we cry "Abba Father!"'. We are able to address God directly and freely as daughters or sons. This freedom underlies Jesus' encouragement to us to ask for anything in his name. 'Anything' sounds extreme, but 'in his name' suggests that we can ask for anything we believe he would want for us. He desires our wholeness in spirit, mind and body and whatever leads to fullness of life for us and others.

3. Our whole being, and certainly our prayer life, can be crippled by feelings of low self worth. It's hard to know where this disease of the mind and spirit comes from. Perhaps it comes from being put down constantly by others or pushed aside as unimportant. Perhaps the relationship with God as it has been taught or caught is one of fear and connected with punishment. 'God won't love you if you do that' or 'You'll go to hell if you commit sin'. Sometimes purity of heart has been confused with sexual purity, so a person may feel quite unacceptable to God because of 'impure' thoughts which are probably part of anyone's sexuality or a healthy sexual development. An excessively puritanical upbringing can lead to all sorts of self deprecation when we find we are not able to live up to the ideals set for us. Jesus offers us forgiveness, freedom from obsessions and a perspective which is able to distinguish between what is important and of lesser importance as far as 'sin' is concerned. Surely he would want us to break that strong nexus established in many minds that sin equals sex and sex equals sin.

4. In the healing ministry we often need to move into the area of human personality. A mind and attitude which

is constantly set on a course of self deprecation, self rejection or self destruction definitely needs healing. This healing may take the form of healing the family tree (this will be dealt with under Question 6) when there may be certain inherited attitudes. Healing of memories may be needed where hurtful things have taken place which have badly affected the self image of the person and their sense of self worth. This is particularly so when physical or emotional abuse has occurred. Sometimes the person has grown up in a dysfunctional family where excessive blame or unhealthy emotional dependence has been rife. Often a whole restructuring of a person's relationships and ways of viewing others needs to be developed. Counselling ministry on a long term basis may be helpful here. Growth in the knowledge of God's grace offered to us in Christ and in the life of the Holy Spirit – the Spirit of truth – will help us along the path to a sense of our worth in God's eyes and value in our own eyes, balanced always with a healthy humility. 'By the grace of God I am what I am'.

For thought and discussion ....

1. 'If the Son shall make you free, you shall be free indeed.' Think of (and share?) some of the freedoms which we can and do experience as believers in Christ.
2. False humility: where have you experienced this in yourself and others?
3. In your experience has sin been equated with sex? What sins may be overlooked or ignored by those obsessed with this equation?
4. How can the 'Spirit of truth' promised by Jesus help us to have a balanced and healthy attitude towards ourselves and our relationships?
5. Ponder the meaning of, and your response to, Paul's question: 'Do you not know that your body is the temple of the Holy Spirit within you?'

STUDY 4:

WHAT DOES IT MEAN TO SAY 'FOR ME TO LIVE IS CHRIST, TO DIE IS GAIN'?

Begin by reading ....

1. Philippians 1:20-26
2. Philippians 2:25-30
3. Matthew 26:36-45 and 27:45,46
4. Romans 14:7-9

Some reflections ....

1. We all have to live with the reality of death about us – our own or the death of others we love. Living in times of lots of medical cures we may not have to confront death for quite large parts of our lives, so it becomes a reality we can keep at arm's length or deny altogether. It's almost an offence to die. In healing ministry circles death is sometimes seen as a failure in our prayer for healing, an evidence of lack of faith. Paul's words 'Whether we live or die, we are the Lord's' help to put things in perspective. He had to live quite large sections of his life with death hanging over his head. In prison in Rome when he wrote to his Philippian friends, members of a church he helped to found and foster, he contemplates the possibility of his own death. He is torn between living and dying – wanting to live on for the sake of his beloved churches only just getting established, but knowing that it would be a joyful experience to die, be with Christ whom he longs for and to be free of his present sufferings. He's caught between the two possibilities. To die is not the ultimate disaster; it can be a definite gain. This thought may be somewhat offensive in our death-denying world.

2. There is fear, grief and anxiety for many of us associated with death, especially untimely death. It may comfort and strengthen us to know that Jesus of Nazareth had these feelings as he faced the possibility of his own suffering and death. In the garden he asked his three close friends to pray and watch with him. He threw himself on the ground and prayed in such agony that, Luke tells us, 'his sweat was like great drops of blood falling down on the ground.' Jesus prayed earnestly for his life to be aligned with the will of God. He drank from the cup given to him; he admitted his flesh was weak though his spirit was willing. We all may have great trouble facing our own death or the death of those close to us. The ministry of family and friends is often to stand with the person as they get over the agonizing hump of acceptance, and to watch with them looking death and its separations in the face. This is often more appropriate ministry than going on praying for physical healing or engaging in death denying behaviour.

3. We all have to live in the circumstances of sickness and health, even of impending death. The apostle Paul was no exception. He gives us glimpses in his Letter to the Philippians of his own feeling when his friend and associate Epaphroditus had been ill and even on the brink of death. 'God had mercy on him, and not only on him but on me also, so that I would not have one sorrow after another.' He sends Epaphroditus back to the Philippians so that they can welcome him with joy – welcome a friend who had come close to death in the midst of his work for Christ. He tells them how anxious he has been, and in a mysterious way his anxiety is lessened by letting them share in it. There is a mutual ministry to one another when we share our anxieties and joys. There is another glimpse we get in the Second Letter to Timothy of Paul's concern for his friends. (see 2 Timothy 1:16-18) In this case the friend, Onesiphorus, who has taken the trouble to seek him out in his imprisonment in Rome and give him some real support, has died. Paul prays for Onesiphorus'

family, remembers with thankfulness his caring, refreshing friendship and commends his soul to God. 'May the Lord grant that he will find mercy from the Lord on that day!' 'In the midst of life we are in death' is the way many funeral services put it. In the ups and downs of life and death we can support and pray for one another. Certainly we do not see death as a failure, nor would we want to deny its reality.

4. In ministry to the seriously ill and their families and friends wisdom is required as to whether to pray for physical healing and build up hopeful expectations in our prayers and believing, or whether to help them prepare for death. We need the guidance of the Holy Spirit and good instincts based upon some experience of ministry. To blunder along as if dying is not an option can have harmful effects. Most dying people and their relatives need someone alongside who can discuss death sensibly and openly with them. A dying person can experience great feelings of isolation and loneliness if they are only surrounded by a cheer-up brigade who refuse to talk about death and its implications. Grief is more complex after death has occurred when the impending death has not been faced openly. It is good to have opportunity to say goodbye and to attend to whatever needs to be done before such a final departure.

For thought and discussion ....

1. From your own experience think of various instances of someone's approaching death and the way it was handled. Were there better ways it could have been done?
2. Someone has said 'Death can be the ultimate healing.' In what ways is this true? When might such a saying be inappropriate?
3. Some people leave instructions about what to do in the case of their death. Discuss the kind of instructions which might be left.
4. There may be some feelings of grief stirred up in you or the group. If appropriate, share these together and pray for one another.

STUDY 5:

FORGIVENESS OF OTHERS IS BASIC TO ALL SPIRITUAL BLESSING. SOMEONE HAS SAID THAT YOU CAN'T FORGIVE IF YOU DON'T HAVE FAITH. DO YOU AGREE WITH THIS?

Begin by reading ....

1. Matthew 18:23-35
2. Colossians 3:13,14
3. Ephesians 4:30-32
4. Hebrews 12:14,15

Some reflections ....

1. In the model prayer which Jesus gave us, it appears that prayer for forgiveness is an essential ingredient. 'Forgive us our sins as we forgive those who sin against us.' The prayer also assumes that we are prepared to forgive others – sometimes a very difficult thing to do. The point of Jesus' parable about the unforgiving servant is that we expect God to forgive us quite big things while often we are intolerantly unforgiving of little things done to us by others. Most of us have a fairly highly developed sense of self-righteousness and are easily hurt and offended. Jesus' spirit is generous and forgiving even towards those who were very deliberately hurting him: 'Father forgive them, for they know not what they do.' Many of our hurts are not even deliberately caused, as we sometimes discover later.

2. Forgiveness is a form of healing: it is inner healing. To know we are forgiven and to be able to forgive are essential

steps on the path to peace of mind and heart. There can be a flow of healing influences in body, mind and spirit when the barriers of unforgiveness and unforgivingness are removed. It is noteworthy that Jesus began his ministry to a paralysed man by declaring that his sins were forgiven: 'Friend, your sins are forgiven you.' This spiritual freedom was then a gateway to physical healing. In healing ministry we do indeed find a strong link between forgiveness and healing. We may even discover that full healing doesn't take place until there is some flow of love and the grace of forgiveness.

3. The writer of the Letter to the Hebrews speaks of the root of bitterness which can spring up in our lives causing trouble for us and our relationships with others. A bitter mind and attitude can imprison us, and twist and distort us. We will never then see the other person clearly and the venom that is in us can poison our mind and spirit, even causing physical ailments and chemical imbalances in our body. The power of God's love shown towards us in the cross of Jesus can accomplish forgiveness in us when we find it hard to do the forgiving ourselves. Jesus cried out from the cross 'It is accomplished!' (the true meaning of 'It is finished!').

   By faith in the Son of God and what he has done for us, we can actually receive the power and strength to love and forgive. The Holy Spirit can create a new mind and spirit in us. The old attitudes die away and, St Paul says, 'everything has become new.'

4. Though there is inestimable power and grace in knowing Jesus Christ – not only his teaching, but his death for us – forgiveness is something which all people can bring about. It is a human resource and it would be wrong to say that only people of religious faith can really forgive. That would be like saying 'Only those who know the love of God can really love.' We are all made in the image of

God, whether we acknowledge that or not and when we forgive and when we love we are exhibiting that God-like character in our humanity. Our experience of life suggests that we can know many people who are not believers who would put many believers to shame, because of the grace that shines through them. It is within the capability of anyone to forgive. Faith in the forgiving, reconciling God revealed to us by Jesus and participation in the life of his Spirit, however, does motivate, empower and inspire forgiveness when it is a more usual human response to take revenge and hold grudges.

For thought and discussion ….

1. In what circumstances is it hard to forgive?
2. How can we draw on Christ's power to forgive and make it our own?
3. Have you encountered non-believers who exhibit grace and forgiveness? What resource do you think they would draw on? How would you commend faith in Christ to them?
4. Share any situations you know of where forgiveness helped to bring about healing in body, mind or spirit.
5. Are there any roots of bitterness in you which may be poisoning your being?

STUDY 6:

IS IT POSSIBLE TO BREAK THE SEQUENCE OF GENERATIONAL PROBLEMS?

Begin by reading ....

1. Exodus 20:4
2. Deuteronomy 28:45,46,58-61
3. Jeremiah 31:29,30
4. John 9:1-3

Some reflections ....

1. Some verses in the Hebrew Scriptures are rather terrifying. Those who know the Ten Commandments well will often have thought of the warning against idolatry in the second Commandment – that those who make for themselves false gods, bow down to them and serve them, are endangering not only themselves but also their descendants 'to the third and fourth generation.' Perhaps lesser known are a series of dire warnings to God's people near the end of the Book of Deuteronomy (a name which means 'the second book of the law'). Moses warns the people of terrible consequences which will flow for them if they forget God and turn away to other gods and follow the abominable practices of their neighbours, such as child sacrifices, ritual prostitution, witchcraft and dealing with the spirits of the dead. The results of their disobedience will be 'among you and your descendants as a sign and a portent forever.' God is depicted as a 'jealous God' with a fierce and passionate love for his people. God does not want to see them fall away from the ways of health, blessing and peace he has laid out for them. God will not willingly surrender his people to other gods and the futile, dangerous and destructive ways associated with them. Hence the dire warnings and the strong language.

2. Have you picked up the counterbalancing promises of blessing in Exodus and Deuteronomy? They are there in abundance. They are not there so much as 'a carrot before the donkey', but as a factual description of what will happen to families and communities if they don't get the basics of faith in the one holy God of the universe and the moral and health codes right. There is a surprisingly dramatic way of translating the positive promise of the second commandment in Exodus 20:4, in the New Revised Standard Version: in contrast to the punishment threatened to descendants to the third and fourth generation, steadfast love is promised 'to the thousandth generation of those who love me and keep my commandments.' The Contemporary English Version (The Bible for Today) follows this meaning also: 'If you love me and obey my laws, I will be kind to your families for thousands of generations.' There are dire consequences for not following God's commandments for sure, but the mercy promised to those who love God and seek to follow the commandments is proportionately greater by far. This gives more than a strong hint of God's amazing love and grace, which we are to discover later in its fullness in Jesus.

3. We should always balance what we find in the Old Testament scriptures with what we find in the New. According to Matthew's Gospel, Jesus said a number of times 'It was said to those of ancient times such and such, but I say to you ….' Jesus restated the law in his own way giving it an even deeper meaning and challenge. However, in the case of sickness being viewed as an inherited punishment, he quite clearly contradicts the traditional understanding. They asked him concerning the man who was born blind – 'Who sinned, this man or his parents, that he was born blind?' Jesus' answer was very definite. 'Neither this man nor his parents sinned; he was born blind so that God's works might be revealed in him.' We do not

believe that sickness is God's punishment, and we seek to be set free from any hint of that. This is a key statement for us in the way we treat the sick or the physically or mentally disabled.

4. We do have to live with a reality that some physical ailments or tendencies towards particular diseases are often part of our inheritance. We would refrain from linking these with Exodus 20:4 or Deuteronomy 28. Such an attitude would be excessively judgmental and un-Christlike. On the other hand we do discover that Jesus healed all kinds of sickness and disease. Matthew in his Gospel makes a number of global statements, observing that every kind of illness and disability was cured by Jesus in his ministry. He records also that Jesus gave authority to his disciples to cast out unclean spirits and to cure every disease and every sickness (see Matthew 10:1). Though it is a great challenge to us and our faith, this suggests that we should believe that he can break the sequence of generational problems, and that we can, in Christ's name and power, set people free from the fear that they will inevitably inherit a particular disease or tendency, or inevitably die at a particular time. Sometimes, the fear of something tends to bring about what we fear. As Job said 'that which I feared greatly has come upon me.' An important ministry is to break that chain of inevitability, and set people free from the fear of it.

For thought and discussion ....

1. Compose a prayer for an imaginary person who is afraid that because their grandparent and/or parent died of a particular disease at approximately the same time in their lives, he or she will suffer the same fate. If you are in a group you may care to share your written prayers and comment on them.
2. Is there some disability or weakness in your family history that you can speak about? A prayer and laying-on-of-hands ministry in the group may be appropriate. Perhaps some private ministry with a minister or counsellor or friend is more appropriate.
3. Discuss Jeremiah's saying about sour grapes and teeth being set on edge, and what this means.
4. Are there dangers in taking biblical texts in isolation? How can we make sure we have a balanced and sensible approach to scripture?

STUDY 7:

CAN A CURSE LAID ON SOMEONE IN THE PAST CAUSE MENTAL ILLNESS LIKE SCHIZOPHRENIA TO AFFLICT MEMBERS OF THE FAMILY IN FUTURE GENERATIONS?

Begin by reading ....

1. If you have not studied Question 6 look at the readings and reflections in relation to that question.
2. Numbers 22.6, 23:11,12
3. Proverbs 27:22-27
4. Galatians 3:10-14
5. James 3:7-18

Some reflections ....

1. 'To curse' is the opposite of 'to bless'. The word 'bless' in New Testament Greek means literally to speak good words towards someone. So to curse is to speak bad and harmful words. It is a power that we have – to call down blessings or to call down curses. In modern Western societies we have a rather casual attitude to words – we throw them about carelessly. We may be sceptical of our power to bless or curse, and somewhat unaware of the power of words. In the readings suggested above you will see that the power of words and of blessings and curses is taken very seriously. The word for 'word' in Hebrew contains the idea of effect; a word is powerful – it does something. 'God said "Let there be light", and there was light', says the Book of Genesis – 'God said .... and it was so.' The Bible speaks not only of the power of God's word but of the power of human words – for good or ill. Reflect for a moment on how much you can be affected

by what another person says – a specialist's diagnosis or a hurtful comment – it goes down deep into the soul. Ancient cultures and religious beliefs take very seriously the power of words and words uttered over persons or objects associated with those persons and we do well to take note. In some cultures it is not uncommon to have a whole pattern of cursing and counter-cursing. If someone is displeased with someone else they go to a person with recognized spiritual power to have a curse laid upon the person they wish to punish. Then that person finds out and gets a counter-curse laid. Much sickness or calamity is explained this way, or responded to this way. In aboriginal societies someone can get sick or even die after the bone has been pointed or a similar ritual engaged in, even in cases where the person doesn't know about it.

2. It would be extremely hurtful and wrong for us to look at a person's mental illness or some other calamity or series of calamities that have befallen them, and assume that a curse has been laid on them or their family. It's not unusual to respond that way – a kind of primitive logic – thinking backwards. On the other hand if we know and have definite evidence that a curse has been laid on a person or family, then we should take action, in Christ's name to break the power of that curse. He, the one who took the things that were against us, and nailed them to the cross, and in that cross triumphed over all spiritualities and powers, as St Paul claims (see Colossians 2:13-15), is able to break the power of curses. God's power of love is stronger – and that is the power revealed and made effective in the world through the life, death and rising again of Jesus.

3. Though we take the power of cursing seriously we are not frightened by it, because we know, through faith and the powerful ministry of prayer of the body of Christ that we can subdue and overcome this power. When we do, we replace it with the power of blessing. We remember Jesus' words

about cleansing a person of evil spirits and evil influences. We are not to leave the house 'swept and garnished' ready for other evil influences to rush in, but to fill the person with the Holy Spirit and encourage them to take positive steps towards the building of a life of prayer and relationship with God in their own right. Their relationships with other people need to be filled with the things that promote blessing. The same principle applies with buildings and places. When it is known that a home or a particular place has been associated with cursing, dabbling with spirits, any kind of abuse or violent and destructive behaviour it is wise to have that place 'cleansed' by prayer. The prayer should include not only driving out harmful influences but also filling the place with God's blessing and covering it with God's protection. Again we find in some cultures a sensitivity to the power of place which is a good reminder to our often sceptical attitudes about such things. We can be strongly influenced by people from the past as well as the present, and we can be influenced, too, by places and their memories and associations for better or for worse.

4. We can be thankful that we live in times where there is a growing understanding of mental illness and especially the illnesses and disorders referred to as schizophrenia. We can be thankful that various therapies and medications have been developed to help people with these disorders. We would see this as God's provision. A good psychiatrist can be truly God's gift to us, helping us with the spiritual and mental distortions which may develop in us. On the other hand we would not dismiss out of hand the lasting and penetrating power of harmful behaviours and words uttered in the past. Ministries of exorcism, the cleansing and blessing of people and places, the laying to rest of troubled spirits and the healing of memories from the past are still appropriate in today's world. We should learn how to use such ministries with responsibility and care.

For thought and discussion ….

1. Think of (and share?) examples of the power of words and their lasting effect, for better or for worse.
2. Discuss the kind of prayer ministry required when we have a friend or member of the family with a mental illness.
3. The blessing and cleansing of buildings and places – has this been an appropriate ministry in your experience? How was it done?
4. 'Mind your language!' Discuss how this warning might apply in our situation.

Bless this house O Lord we pray,
make it safe by night and day.

STUDY 8:

WHAT PART DOES DISCERNMENT PLAY IN HEALING PRAYER?

Begin by reading ....

1. 1 Corinthians 12:7-11
2. 1 Kings 3:3-14
3. 1 Corinthians 2:6-16
4. Hebrews 4:12,13

Some reflections ....

1. Paul mentions 'discernment of spirits' as one of the gifts of the Spirit. This probably refers to the ability to distinguish between what comes from God and what comes from another source – an evil spirit or some form of human trickery or counterfeit. From earliest times it seems that there were those who, through a desire to take the place of God or deliberately to deceive, presumed to speak with the voice of God or to exercise spiritual power for their own purposes. In the Acts of the Apostles we read of the Sons of Sceva (Acts 19:11-20) who tried to cast out evil spirits using Jesus' name, but not being themselves committed followers of Jesus. Wherever healing ministry is practised there needs to be some caution exercised by those in leadership, in fact by all present, to make sure that God is being served, not human glorification. There may be a temptation to claim more than should be claimed, because a particular minister's reputation, or ministry's reputation, is at stake. Jesus himself warned about false Messiahs and false prophets whom he likened to wolves in sheep's clothing. The gift of discernment is needed to test the genuineness of spiritual gifts and ministries. This gift can also help us identify and name any troublesome spirits or painful experiences of the past that may be interfering in a person's life, causing obsessions or addictions, or

excessive fears. It is a diagnostic gift, helping us to see what lies beneath the surface – the hidden factors.

2. Close to discernment is the gift of wisdom. Paul speaks of a word of wisdom as a gift of the Spirit. It comes first in his list of gifts. We certainly need wisdom as well as discernment when we pray for another person, especially when the prayer is public. Sometimes the person being prayed for hears a word of wisdom in the prayer uttered or in a comment made by a friend. This word of wisdom then helps the person to embark on a wise course of action or a new way of seeing a person or a problem. This writer went forward in a healing service for relief of indigestion which had become severe over a period of time. A very brief prayer was uttered as hands were laid on – 'Lord guide Owen in his lifestyle.' This wise word sunk in. I discussed the problem with my family and we made some changes, including not answering the phone at meal times. Eventually the indigestion went away.

3. Wisdom and discernment are needed as we minister to others. Is our prayer pastorally appropriate? Does our ministry leave room for the person to take responsibility for themselves? Are we exposing the person and their situation to others in an unhealthy way? Are we being too 'heavy' in our approach? Is the grace and love of God being exhibited in what we are doing? Questions like these are helpful checks to our ministry. Ministry can sometimes be invasive and abusive where wisdom is lacking. In the Second Letter to Timothy a good combination of gifts is mentioned – power, love and sound-mindedness (see 2 Timothy 1:7). Sound-mindedness is being wise and balanced. Power always needs to be combined with love or it can be an ugly thing. Both power and love need to be tempered by wisdom and practical common sense.

4. The writer of the Letter to the Hebrews (we do not know who this is) speaks of the word of God being able to discern our inmost thoughts and motives. I know that many would think that the word of God is the scriptures. Bear in mind, however, that the word of God is a communication from God. Jesus is described by John as 'the word of God made flesh', a living word rather than a written word. The scriptures contain the record of what he said and did, and accounts of how God has communicated with his people in history. Jesus did indeed have a discerning and wise mind. He seemed to be able to cut through to what was true or untrue. He exercised gifts of the Spirit – a word of wisdom or knowledge, gifts of healing all kinds of diseases and discerning harmful spirits. We can see that he did know, in a surefooted way, how to minister to people and what was happening in their inner being. John commented that he knew what was in the human heart. In the ministry of healing we seek to connect with Jesus and his way of doing things. We minister, as we say, 'in his name'. If there isn't some discernment and wisdom in what we do and how we pray, then we may wonder if we are really in touch with him and his Spirit, and whether we are doing things only according to our own understanding. Healing prayer most definitely needs to be led by the Spirit, the Spirit of wisdom and discernment.

For thought and discussion ....

1. Think of (and share?) any time when a wise or discerning word has come to you or your healing group or church community.
2. In what circumstances can prayer or ministry be harmful?
3. How can we achieve the balance referred to in 2 Timothy 1:7 – power, love and a sound mind?
4. Compose a prayer for wisdom and discernment in your life and ministry. Perhaps these prayers can be shared around the group.

STUDY 9:

WHY DOESN'T THE CHURCH ALWAYS ENCOURAGE HEALING MINISTRY, SEEING IT IS SUCH A LARGE PART OF JESUS' MINISTRY?

Begin by reading ....

1. Luke 10:1-9
2. John 20:19-23
3. Acts 4:21-31
4. 1 Corinthians 12:27-31

Some reflections ....

1. It seems clear from the New Testament that Jesus got his reputation not only for being a great teacher, but also because of his healing ministry. Crowds gathered from near and far to hear him and witness his amazing acts of healing. It is also clear from all four gospels that he commissioned his disciples to preach and heal in his name. In Luke's Gospel it is clear that it is not only the twelve disciples he commissioned in this way, but a wider group of followers. His words uttered at the time of his resurrection, according to John, give the same impression: 'As the Father sent me, so I send you.' Some Christians believe that all this is indeed true, but that miracles of healing only belong to New Testament times – that they were given by God to attest to the truth of the gospel, and not intended to be repeated in the life of the church. The great reformer John Calvin wrote: 'The gift of healing disappeared with the other miraculous powers which the Lord was pleased to give for a time, that it might render the new preaching of the gospel for ever wonderful.' Yet if we take the doctrine of the body of Christ seriously and

what Jesus said and did according to the gospel writers, it seems more likely that he intended his followers in all times and places to have the authority to heal in his name. From time to time in the history of the church, especially in times of renewal and revival, this power to heal in Jesus' name has come up again in the life of the church. Some of us have witnessed many and varied healings when prayer for healing and ministries of laying on of hands and anointing have been carried out in faith. To quote Peter's words: 'We cannot but speak of what we have seen and heard.'

2. Perhaps there is something tied up in expectations. If we have no expectation of healing happening as the result of prayer and ministry, little healing may take place. If we have expectations and exercise faith in the living God and his power to bring healing in body, mind and spirit, we may open ourselves and others up to receiving blessing and healing. Not always does physical cure take place, but there are other areas of being where healing can take place – peace of mind and spirit, the healing of relationships or the diminishing of fear.

3. There is a worry on the part of some churches and some believers that through the healing ministry people will be given false expectations, and only face disappointment or loss of faith when healing does not take place. Some have experienced condemnation for lack of faith when they or their relatives or friends haven't been healed: 'You didn't have enough faith.' 'You didn't trust God enough.' 'There were barriers in you preventing healing.' This kind of condemnation certainly is very hurtful. Many churches too, quite rightly, want to emphasise the importance of medical science in bringing healing. Some people say that we don't need the healing ministry of the church any more because we are provided with good medical care and helpful medicines. A wise approach is 'both and' rather than 'either or'. We thank God for the gifts of medical

science and research and his provision of good doctors and specialists. We honour them and pray for the success of their work. We also engage in the prayer of faith and ministries of healing for the sick so that, with the stirring of faith and the receiving of proper medical attention, God's purposes of healing and wholeness might be achieved. A narrow and exclusive approach by some who are zealous for the healing ministry, even suggesting that people throw away their medicines, forsake their doctors and rely only on faith, has created some suspicions and reservations concerning the healing ministry on the part of some churches.

4. As mentioned in Chapter 8, reflection 1, some discernment is needed to determine whether a particular ministry is pastorally appropriate for the person receiving it. To go on holding out the hope for physical healing when it would be better to engage in a ministry of preparation for death is irresponsible. It is an invitation to the person and their family to engage in denial and can have very serious pastoral consequences. In the same way, wise discernment is needed as to when to be cautious about claiming physical healing and when to be bold. We also need to be able to distinguish between boldness and presumption. There may be good reason for churches to be cautious about people who claim too much or set unrealistic expectations. When all is said and done, however, it would be a pity for churches or individual believers to refrain from engaging in the prayer of faith for healing or public ministries of healing just because of distortions or false claims which may have been engaged in from time to time. We can be too cautious and too timorous, too influenced by the negatives. Perhaps we should recall Jesus' words to his somewhat hesitant disciples: 'Launch out into the deep ....' and 'if you have faith, even the size of a mustard seed, you will say to this mountain "Move from here to there", and it will move; and nothing will be impossible for you.'

For thought and discussion ….

1. Church leaders have a responsibility to protect their members from false teachings and misleading claims. What advice would you give to your church leaders as to how they handle the claims of the healing ministry?
2. Have you encountered people who have been hurt by inappropriate ministry in the area of healing or dealing with death? Why did the hurts occur and what could have been done to avoid them?
3. Think about (and discuss?) the tension between caution and boldness
   (a) in your own life and
   (b) in the church's witness.
4. How can we best encourage a complementary approach between the church's healing ministry and medical practice?

STUDY 10:

WHY ME?

Begin by reading ....

1. Job 10
2. Psalm 22
3. Jeremiah 20
4. 2 Corinthians 4

Some reflections ....

1. Prayer takes many forms – thanksgiving, adoration, confession and intercession. One of the forms of prayer not uncommon in the Bible is the prayer of complaint. Why have you done this to me? Why is your hand heavy upon me? Why do you seem so far off? Why did you bring me forth from the womb? We can certainly understand Jesus on the cross crying out to God in agony and desolation, and using the opening words of Psalm 22 – 'My God, my God, why have you forsaken me?' It is part of the good news of the gospel that Jesus shared our full humanity, even to the point of wondering 'Why?' We shouldn't stifle complaints, nor should we be afraid of addressing them to God. It may help us to express the pain and distress of our soul. In the Book of Job we find that his friends who gather to comfort him only argue against his complaints and tell him, unhelpfully, that he must have sinned against God. They say he must not complain against God's righteousness and justice. Job's anguish is only increased. Who wants super-pious, self-righteous preachers around when one is complaining? A listening ear and an understanding heart is what is needed, and an ability to sit with the person in their darkness.

2. The question 'Why me?' with the emphasis on the 'me' implies that the questioner thinks he or she is being unjustly treated by God. As mentioned in earlier studies,

there is a natural human reaction to sickness or adversity – to think that it is a punishment sent by God. The old Church of England Book of Common Prayer included the following words in the service of The Visitation of the Sick: 'Take therefore in good part the chastisement of the Lord: for whom the Lord loveth he chasteneth, and scourgeth every son whom he receiveth.' Ironically, the words originally come from the words of one of Job's 'comforters', Eliphaz the Temanite. It is unlikely that even the most ardent traditionalist would be helped and comforted by those words today. However, we can understand that in the light of such heavy handed 'pastoral care' people have indeed thought of their sickness as punishment and chastisement from God. Jesus' words and attitude seem to be quite different. He spoke of the universal nature of God's provision – 'he makes it rain on both the just and the unjust' - and the lack of connection between what happens to us and what we deserve or don't deserve. He spoke of the Galileans who had suffered at the hands of Pontius Pilate: 'Do you think that because these Galileans suffered in this way they were worse sinners than all other Galileans? .... Or those eighteen who were killed when the tower of Siloam fell on them – do you think that they were worse offenders than all the others living in Jerusalem?' (see Luke 13:1-5) Jesus then goes on to suggest that as we contemplate the fact that anything can happen to us without any apparent reason or explanation we all need to repent before God, not just some who are supposedly more wicked than others. Part of human life is sharing in calamities and tragedies and living in a world of chance and accident. No one is exempt from this reality.

3. People may have difficulty reconciling belief in God's providence and sovereignty with the realities of life and its apparently random happenings. It is hard for us to see the overall picture; one day we believe we will. Paul speaks of the groaning and travailing of creation and its 'not yet' quality. Jesus told his parable about the wheat and the

weeds being left to grow together until harvest. Things are not yet sorted out. The universe seems to have a life of its own and some independence of its creator. Just as we are given freedom, perhaps it is of the very nature of creation likewise to have some freedom. We should refrain from saying 'This is the will of God' when human beings do something really dreadful, which is clearly contrary to the will of God. Likewise we would hesitate to speak of a natural disaster such as an earthquake as the will of God or a way of punishing those who have sinned. Pandemics such as Aids are not scourges sent from God. Yet we dare to believe in God's overarching providence and care for us. We dare to believe that there is no circumstance of life where God cannot help us to bring something good or noble out of what has happened. It is best to avoid simplistic explanations and conclusions. With God's help, we commit ourselves to redeeming each situation we are confronted with, seeking to bring the best out of it. God gives us a part in the working out of his overall purpose and a stewardship of care for others and the creation in all its delicate checks and balances.

4. In the face of the enormous and puzzling questions of life, the cry 'Why me?' seems a little too self-centred, though it is understandable in the midst of calamity. The bitterness behind it may prevent us from moving on and making decisions about what needs to be done in the circumstances. It would be a mark of maturity in us to be able to say to God 'Help me to grasp this situation and handle it in a way that will be best for me and for others, and will glorify you.'

For thought and discussion ....

1. Think about (and discuss?) the appropriate way of responding to someone who is questioning 'Why me?"
2. How do we break the connection in people's minds between sickness and punishment?
3. Share any examples or stories from your experience of victims of sickness, accidents and other tragedies, moving on from the bitterness of 'Why me?' to more positive attitudes.
4. Perhaps we should be careful about our use of the expression 'it must be God's will' in relation to happenings which have bad consequences for ourselves or for others. Discuss whether you agree or not with this statement.

STUDY 11:

IS IT A SIN TO WANT TO DIE?

Begin by reading ....

1. Psalm 90:9,10,12
2. Psalm 31:13-15
3. Ecclesiastes 3:1-8
4. Romans 8:35-39

Some reflections ....

1. Euthanasia is such a hot subject in the community and in the churches in our times that it is hard to respond coolly to the question before us. Yet if we listen carefully to the question, we notice that the questioner is asking whether it is a sin to <u>want</u> to die. How could it be? In that case Paul must have sinned in saying that he was caught between living and dying; he thought it was far better to depart and be with Christ (see Philippians 1:20-24). No, it is quite appropriate for a suffering person to want to die. A believer has faith that he or she will be with Christ who has gone to prepare a place for us - 'If it were not so, I would have told you' Jesus said. Some of us have been with dying people and their relatives and friends who are longing for death to come, and praying for it to come. Sometimes it is hard to die. As well as that, there is a strong tendency to prolong life at all costs in modern medical practice. Life-saving drugs are administered and life support systems kept on when the long term, or even the short term, prognosis is very poor. There's a time to live and a time to die, and we need the wisdom to tell the difference, and the courage to make the right medical decisions.

2. Many believers would strongly reject such intervention as would deliberately bring about death. 'My times are in your hands' is a poignant way of expressing our faith and trust in God. We may have the life long habit of commending

ourselves into God's hands every night: 'Father into your hands I commend my spirit.' When the time is right, God will take us, and we are content with that. We may indeed feel that to terminate deliberately our own life or that of another is taking the issues of life and death into our own hands – playing God, as it were. Yet in modern medical practice there is much intervention, and there are many life and death decisions, sometimes very risky decisions, which have to be made. The issues are not necessarily clear cut, and ethicists are called in to help make judgments about them. It is not unusual for a family to have to make a solemn decision as to when a life support system should be turned off or a particular medical treatment terminated. Sometimes life and death decisions are in our hands. This could be seen as a stewardship committed to us by God. May God give us wisdom and right judgment when we are faced with such decisions.

3. It is not uncommon for people to want to die because of a state of mind which has developed in them. Suicide and attempted suicide are at problematic levels in contemporary society. Rather than being judgmental about it and talking about 'sin' it is better for us to seek to understand why this is so, and to help our community and our churches to develop some preventative strategies. Thoughts of suicide often accompany depressive episodes in a person's life, so the healing of people with depressive illnesses should be the concern of medical science and the churches in their healing ministries. The spiritual component of a person's life and outlook is highly relevant. Helping people to have positive attitudes about themselves and their future and to be healed of self-destructive and self-punishing urges is a task for the healing ministry and of faith communities in general. The words of Jeremiah come to mind: 'Surely I know the plans I have for you, says the Lord, plans for your welfare and not for harm, to give you a future and a hope.' (see Jeremiah 29:11) Our ministry is to help people grasp hope when they are tempted to despair. In

the face of a sense of failure which is hard to deal with it is good if the person can talk about it with someone. A lot of suicides happen in circumstances where feelings are not shared. Men in particular may find it difficult to talk with someone and admit to their problems. In a competitive culture where everyone has to be a success in what they do some find seeming failure almost impossible to deal with. In the rearing of children we need to help them deal with failures or perceived lack of success as part of normal living. Academic failure, business failure, marriage failure and farming failure are some of the circumstances that may trigger thoughts of suicide. The ability to let past failures or disappointments go and not be obsessed by them is something we all need to develop. A church or family climate where people are not able to share and deal with shame and failure is not helpful; it is in fact positively harmful. Perhaps we should allow others to see more of our less successful side, more of our vulnerability.

4. As far as euthanasia is concerned, we will not be able to avoid debate about it. In all likelihood the community will press for appropriate legislation and members of the churches will need to know where they stand. Already there is considerable disagreement about it across our country, and no doubt across our churches. It is not the place of this study to take up a position about it, but to encourage earnest discussion and thought. Certainly the unnecessary prolongation of life is not helpful, so there can be a strong argument in favour of what is sometimes called 'passive euthanasia'. This refers to removing the pressure on doctors to keep the patient alive at all costs. Active euthanasia raises lots of questions – will older people feel under pressure to do away with themselves in order not to be a nuisance to others? This is a strong motivation on the part of some. Palliative care is also a provision for us to allow us to have an almost pain-free death. The fear of what might happen to us on the way to death is sometimes much greater than the reality. Some of

us may definitely prefer to stay with the psalmist in saying 'My times are in your hand', rather than taking them into our own hand.

For thought and discussion ....

1. The church's history of dealing with suicide deaths is somewhat harsh – suicides were not allowed to be buried in consecrated burial grounds, nor was the full Christian Burial Service said over them. What is your reaction to this tradition? Is there a better way and are we following it?
2. Think about (and discuss?) your stance over both passive and active euthanasia. Perhaps your group could have such a discussion, making sure different points of view are presented.
3. How can we best help people with suicidal thoughts? What ministries of the church can be helpful in this area?
4. How might we help people, ourselves included, deal with the fear of death or what precedes death?

STUDY 12:

WHAT PART DOES ANOINTING PLAY IN HEALING MINISTRY? WHEN SHOULD IT BE USED AND BY WHOM?

Begin by reading ....

1. Exodus 30:22-32
2. Isaiah 61:1-4
3. Mark 6:12,13
4. James 5:13-16

Some reflections ....

1. In the Hebrew tradition anointing is associated with consecrating holy persons and holy places. It was used also to consecrate kings to stress that they had a God-given and God-appointed leadership. In Isaiah 61, a text that Jesus read in the local synagogue of Nazareth and applied to himself, there is an anointed leader sent by God to bring deliverance and all kinds of healing. Whenever the title 'Christ' or 'Messiah' is used with reference to Jesus it has the meaning of 'the anointed one of God'. We see him as a king, a priest, a healer and a deliverer – not perhaps in the way envisaged by the people looking for a Messiah who would deliver them from the power of Rome and set up an earthly Jewish Kingdom. Rather he is the one chosen, anointed and empowered by God to bring all the peoples of the world to wholeness and to establish a spiritual kingdom where God would rule in all parts of life. It is not surprising that Jesus Christ, the anointed one, should use anointing as one of the outward signs of the accomplishment of his healing purposes. There is only one reference in the gospels to the practice of anointing the sick with oil, backed up of course, by the advice in

James' Letter that the sick should call for the elders of the church and that they should anoint them and pray the prayer of faith over them. Clearly anointing with oil was one of the outward signs of healing in the early Christian community and has been, in some branches of the church, ever since.

2. For some centuries in the Roman Catholic tradition anointing was used for the dying, in preparing them for death and giving the promise of ultimate healing in God's presence. Fortunately over the past fifty or sixty years Holy Unction or anointing has been restored as a sign of healing for the sick, as was originally intended. The churches of the Reformation tended to be very cautious about sacramental signs other than those of Baptism and Holy Communion, and didn't practise anointing of the sick. Over the past century, however, anointing has been restored in the life of many churches along with the practice of laying hands on the sick. We can be thankful for the renewal of this scripturally based and richly symbolic ministry to the sick.

3. Jesus clearly made strong use of outward signs in his own ministry. His actions spoke as strongly as his words. We might think of Jesus putting his fingers in the ears of a deaf man with a speech impediment and spitting and touching his tongue with his saliva. Jesus said simply 'Be opened' (see Mark 7:31-37). This was clearly an effective way of ministering to such a person, especially as saliva was understood, quite correctly, to be a healing agent. Jesus also used saliva as he made some mud and anointed the eyes of a man who had been blind from birth (see John 9:6). The outward sign here was rich in meaning, reminding the onlookers of God's work of creation and re-creation. Though outward signs may not, strictly speaking, be necessary, they certainly help to stir faith in the person being healed and in the onlookers. It is the same in the case of anointing with olive oil. Oil reminds us of ointment,

and has been a symbol since ancient times to signify the flow of God's blessing. Laying on of hands gives a similar connotation: the person is being blessed by the faith community. The use of the outward signs blended with simple prayers of faith helps to stir faith. Jesus Christ is the anointed one of God who anoints for healing. We become the anointed community who anoint in his name, as he told us to do.

4. Anointing often brings deep peace and inward as well as outward healing to a person: 'As your body is outwardly anointed with this visible oil, so may our heavenly Father grant you the inward anointing of the Holy Spirit. With his great mercy, may he forgive you your sins, release you from suffering and restore you to wholeness and strength.' (from the Order of St Luke the Physician Handbook). We use anointing when the Christian Community is officially gathered to pray for a person's healing in body, mind and spirit. Usually it is followed by the laying on of hands by members of the gathered community. The oil is blessed and set apart for healing. In some churches this is done by the bishop to signify that this is a ministry of the whole church community. Anointing is carried out only by ordained ministers or elders in some churches and in other churches members who are called to special ministries of healing are authorized to anoint. It is best to be clear that this is an authorized and official ministry with the backing of the church community, rather than the action of an isolated individual.

For thought and discussion ....

1. Share any experience of anointing for healing you have had, or know others have had, when beneficial results have followed.
2. The anointed one anoints. Think about (and discuss?) the meaning of this statement in relation to (a) Jesus, (b) the church and (c) those commissioned to heal.
3. Why do you think there may be more power in the gathered community's ministry of healing, than in one individual's ministry? Read and discuss Matthew 18:18-20.
4. Do you find the outward sign of anointing helpful? If so, why, and if not, why not?

STUDY 13:

IS IT A VALID MINISTRY TO CAST OUT EVIL SPIRITS? HOW IS IT DONE?

Begin by reading ....

1. Deuteronomy 18:9-14
2. 1 Samuel 28:3-25
3. Mark 5:1-5
4. Ephesians 6:10-18

Some reflections ....

1. In our times people may be very cautious indeed of speaking about 'evil spirits'. Many would be sceptical even of accepting the notion of the Holy Spirit. Those of us who are Christian believers attest to the presence of the Holy Spirit as promised by Jesus – 'he abides with you and will be in you' (see John 14:17). We are also aware of the influence of a contrary spirit which, after Jesus' example, we refer to as the devil or Satan. Whether or not we name or personify that rebellious anti-God spirit, its power is to be taken seriously and resisted. Paul tells us that we have to wrestle not against flesh and blood, but against powers that he describes as 'the spiritual forces of evil in the heavenly places.' Our struggle against evil forces requires God's armour and protection and the lifelong task of equipping ourselves properly for that struggle. Satan is described in the scriptures as an angel or spirit who has rebelled against God and who tries to stir up opposition to God and enlist people in the service of evil rather than the service of God. Satan is described as an accuser – the false accuser of the people of God, always undermining and deceiving. Those who make significant steps of faith or those who set out quite consciously to serve God in some ministry to which they are called do experience

strong discouragement both from within themselves and in outward circumstances; they do not find it hard to speak of the tempter, accuser or discourager in personal terms, as if he has a particular interest in thwarting God's purposes and God's people. Peter's Letter which speaks of our 'adversary the devil roving around like a roaring lion' tells us to resist him from a position of steadfast faith (see 1 Peter 5:8,9), while James' Letter says: 'Resist the devil and he will flee from you' (see James 4:7).

2. We can influence other people for better or for worse. It is as if our spirit is catching. Laughter and joy are catching; so are fear and an attitude of defeat. Our spirits communicate with one another. It is good to be surrounded by people whose spirits are positive and depressing to be surrounded by those whose spirits are excessively negative. Believers pray for one another in a positive spirit of faith which is the gift of God's Holy Spirit, and we believe that in life beyond death in God's presence we will go on praying for our friends. The Letter to the Hebrews speaks of us being 'encompassed with a great cloud of witnesses' who pray for us and encourage us as we run the race of this life (see Hebrews 12:1). We call this surrounding company 'the communion of saints'. Some spirits, however, may not be happy to leave this world, or perhaps have not been released and commended to God. It is possible that they 'stay about', as we might say, and cause disturbance. For centuries the church has known that particular places or people can be troubled by spirits who have no peace, and rituals have been used to bless places and cleanse them of any troubled or troublesome spirits. Many people have been convinced of the validity of this ministry when it has been found that after a service of blessing and cleansing the troublesome influences have gone and peace has been restored.

3. The practice of trying to get in touch with departed spirits through séances or mediums is condemned in the

scriptures and treated as forbidden by most Christians. The passage about Saul seeking to call up the spirit of his departed mentor Samuel through the woman at Endor who was a medium, has the ring of authenticity about it. Samuel is not happy at all about being 'called up' and Saul is completely demolished by knowing his future. We do well not to dabble in fortune-telling or occult practices. Knowing our future may only depress us and dispose us towards suffering what is predicted. In any case the prediction may be the work of a lying, deceitful spirit. Those with experience in ministries of deliverance from evil spirits find that a history of occult involvement is the precursor to a spiritually troubled or mentally disturbed life. Quite drastic consequences such as nightmares, behavioural disorders or suicide can follow. Just as we were reminded in the last paragraph that if we resist the devil he will flee from us, the opposite is probably true. Invite the devil or any spirits other than the Holy Spirit into our lives and they will take up residence and cause significant trouble.

4. The Lord's Prayer has one petition out of seven devoted to the request for God to deliver us from evil. The word 'evil' can be translated as 'the evil one'. Jesus, who himself wrestled with the devil and his temptations, not only in the forty days when he was out in the wilderness, but at other times in his life and ministry, clearly treated deliverance from evil as a valid part of prayer and ministry. A number of Jesus' acts of healing could be described as deliverance ministries. He cast out evil spirits and brought wholeness and peace. He pictured himself as 'binding the strong man and plundering his property' – in other words releasing those who were captive to Satan (see Matthew 12:29). However it would be wrong for us to focus too much on deliverance as if every sickness or every human trouble were caused by evil spirits. Such an emphasis would be unhealthy and diminish our own sense of responsibility for the matters over which we have choice and control. James wisely advises us not to keep saying, as it were,

‘the devil made me do it’ and certainly not to say ‘I am being tempted by God.’ ‘One is tempted by one’s own desire, being lured and enticed by it.’ (see James 1:14) From time to time, but not often, we are confronted by a person who has been subject to evil spirits – usually when they have surrendered themselves to such influence or deliberately engaged in Satanic rituals. A strong, wise, loving and non-fearful ministry is required with definite commands in the Lord’s name for Satan or any spirits that are not of God to depart. We tell them to go under Christ’s authority to the place of spirits, and not to trouble the person or their surroundings any more.

Cautionary Note: This ministry should be conducted with the knowledge and authorization of the church leadership; it should be done in the presence of several people, preferably those with some experience in deliverance ministry and discernment of spirits and with strong coverage with prayer before, during and after such ministry. It is best done semi-privately so as not to stir up fear or fuss. Why should we give publicity to spirits who frequently turn on some rather dramatic histrionics? There is often an unhealthy curiosity about this ministry which is best not encouraged. Strict confidentiality is needed to protect the person being ministered to. Deliverance ministry should be followed by anointing, Holy Communion and prayer that any empty place in the person should be filled with God’s love and presence. Extreme care should be taken with those suffering from mental illness or those under treatment for such illness. We would not want to undermine treatment already being received nor to put suggestions in people’s minds that they are infected with evil spirits by ministering to them using words which imply that. Distinguishing between truth and delusion is an important aspect of this ministry. Sometimes it is the delusion itself which may be from an unhealthy spiritual source. Fortunately the Holy Spirit is the Spirit of truth!

For thought and discussion ....

1. Think about (and discuss?) the dangers of (a) over-emphasis and (b) under-emphasis on deliverance ministry within the overall context of the healing ministry.
2. Do you know of people who have been the subject of deliverance ministry? Without divulging any confidential matters unless authorized to do so by the person concerned, relate to the group the benefits (or bad effects) of this ministry.
3. Much has been spoken and written of poltergeist activity in buildings or places associated with people now deceased. What do you make of this? Do you have any particular experiences to relate? Is there a ministry of cleansing and blessing of such places offered by your church community?
4. The Church of England (in England) has issued guidelines relating to exorcism. A specialist person is appointed by the bishop in each diocese of the church and no exorcisms are to be conducted without consultation with that person. Some consultation with a doctor (or psychiatrist) in every case is required (or strongly advised). Discuss whether you think these are wise provisions.

STUDY 14:

WHAT ROLE DOES PAIN PLAY IN OUR LIVES? HOW SHOULD WE DEAL WITH IT IN THE HEALING MINISTRY?

Begin by reading ....

1. Psalm 38
2. Isaiah 53:4-12
3. Mark 15:16-39
4. 1 Peter 4:12-19

Some reflections ....

1. The psalms, and for that matter the scriptures in general, include pain and suffering in the range of human experience which is described and encompassed in God's work of redemption. On this basis, it would not be right for any believer to feel that they should be exempt, or divinely protected, from human pain. Christ wasn't, nor were the saints of God. It sounds as if Psalm 38 is the prayer of a grievously sick person. Very real pain is vividly described – like arrows deliberately aimed and sticking deep in the flesh. There is emotional pain described there too: 'My friends and companions stand aloof from my affliction, and my neighbours stand far off.' One is reminded of the sufferings of Job, who not only suffered greatly in his dreadful sickness, but had to endure the pious exhortations of his friends who told him he must have sinned and should repent. 'Miserable comforters are you all!' cries out Job in his suffering (see Job 16:2). There is some evidence that Psalm 38 was used regularly in the temple worship. Perhaps it was there so that any sick or hurt person could use it as a vehicle of worship – a cry to God out of the genuine experience of pain, both spiritual and physical.

It is well if our worship contains some lament as well as praise; we are not always in a place of rejoicing.

2. Physical pain is, of course, a signal to us that something is wrong in our body. Those who lose the sense of feeling in any part of their body are actually in danger – they may hurt or injure themselves without knowing it and all kinds of dreadful consequences may follow. So pain is a wise provision for us. We then seek help from the physician or the pharmacist who are described in Sirach 38 (one of the books of the Apocrypha) as God's gift to us – 'the sensible will not despise them.' Sometimes, however, the physician cannot diagnose what is wrong, nor can medicines be devised which give relief. Sufferers of acute and continuous pain certainly deserve our understanding, our sympathy and strong prayer support. Long nights of pain must be almost unbearable. We can be thankful that the developments in palliative medicine in our own times have brought relief to many sufferers of acute pain. There are still some, however, whose pain seems to be beyond the reach of human help. They should always be included in our intercessory prayer. In the practice of Christian healing ministry, it is not unknown for a person who has been anointed or had hands laid on them with the prayer of faith to be relieved of pain. Such ministry can, it would seem, speak to the deep places in the brain or the psyche, and the mountain of pain can be removed. The focus of prayer should sometimes be just that – the removal of pain. Agreed and focussed prayer is of more effect than generalized prayer. By 'agreed prayer' we mean that a number of people pray the prayer of faith perhaps at the same time or regularly at a given time, and by 'focussed prayer' we mean having a specific end in mind, such as the removal of pain from a particular part of the body, the shrinking of a tumour, the release of a frozen shoulder, or whatever.

3. When Peter's Letter speaks of Christians enduring 'the fiery trial' and rejoicing 'as you are sharing Christ's sufferings', this is almost certainly a reference to enduring persecutions and discouragements as a result of being Christ's followers and witnesses. The 'fiery trial' (Authorized Version) is translated in the New International Version as 'painful suffering'. It is the same expression as Jesus used in the Lord's Prayer where it is often translated as 'save us from the time of trial' rather than 'lead us not into temptation'. Christians have often applied this 'painful suffering' to the suffering of sickness, though this is not what was originally meant. Suffering, as it is understood and spoken of in the New Testament, refers more particularly to the persecution, opposition and indignities suffered by Christ's followers. Paul speaks of making up in his own flesh what is lacking in Christ's sufferings for the sake of his body, the church (see Colossians 1:24). There has been much debate over this rather bold verse. He suggests that there is a complement of suffering to be yet filled up by the church, Christ's suffering body, and that he and we are part of that. In another place he speaks of 'the fellowship of Christ's sufferings' and becoming 'like him in his death' (see Philippians 3:10). Though the primary meaning of suffering here is not sickness, it is helpful to include our way of dealing with sickness, its pains, discouragements and traumas, as a 'fiery trial' that we go through in fellowship with Christ who suffered for us. 'He took our infirmities and carried our diseases' (see Isaiah 53:4 and Matthew 8:17).

4. Over the centuries of Christian faith and ministry exhortations have been given to the sick to offer up their sickness in union with Christ's sacrifice and sufferings. In Catholic hospitals it has been usual to have a crucifix in each room to help people do this. A teaching was developed that as we suffered pain with Christ so we were joining with him in his work of redemption. Paul's teaching seems to imply this (see 2 Corinthians 1:5-7).

The suffering Christian emphasis can, however be taken to extremes – 'suffering, suffering, cross, cross – that is the Christian's only right' said Martin Luther. (Admonition to Peace, 1525).

When applied to sickness, such an approach can discourage people from seeking healing. 'This sickness, this suffering, must be God's will for me.' We notice that it was not Jesus' way of dealing with people. He did speak of enduring torture, betrayal, hatred, the increase of lawlessness, the love of many growing cold and many falling away from faith (see Matthew 24:9-13), but not of enduring sickness in a stoical way. Rather he brought healing and relief. The emphasis in James' Letter is that if we are suffering from sickness and pain, we should call for the elders of the church to pray over us, anointing us with oil in the name of the Lord, and exercising the prayer of faith for us. We can take the positive approach and beware of any withering violet, this-must-be-God's-will-for-me-approach, which excludes asking for help. It is better to go to the doctor, get relief from pain and ask for prayer and ministry to help you. If there is enduring pain and suffering, if our body baffles medical science, and there appears to be no answer to prayer, then surely we can offer that suffering to God. We can ask for the attitude of mind that Paul took when his repeated prayer was not answered. He heard the Lord say to him 'My grace is sufficient for you and my strength is made perfect in weakness' (see 2 Corinthians 12:7-10). Though almost certainly not referring to sickness in this place, the attitude of mind and spirit which Paul describes can help to carry us through.

For thought and discussion ....

1. Have you suffered extreme physical or emotional pain in your life? How was it dealt with? Share your experience with other members of the group if you are able and it is appropriate.
2. There are a number of psalms of lament in the Psalter. Find and read one other than Psalm 38. What place might lament have in the church's worship? What place does it have in your church?
3. 'Job's comforters' – discuss the dangers of falling into this role. How do we avoid it?
4. What do you think it means to talk of 'the fellowship of Christ's suffering' (as expressed in Philippians 3:10)?

STUDY 15:

IN WHAT WAYS CAN SICKNESS BE A BENEFIT TO US? IF IT IS OF BENEFIT, WHY SHOULD I PRAY FOR HEALING?

Begin by reading ....

1. Psalm 103
2. Isaiah 38:9-20
3. Daniel 4:28-37
4. Acts 3:1-16

Some reflections ....

1. Part of our maturity as persons, our humanity, is having to deal with calamities and sickness. Those who have never had to deal with such things may lack a depth in their being. When we are looking for someone to talk with and to share some of our troubles with, we do well to choose a person who has had some experience of adversity. The poet, Gerard Manley Hopkins wrote:

   'O the mind, mind has mountains, cliffs of fall
   Frightful, sheer, no-man-fathomed. Hold them cheap
   May who ne'er hung there.'
   from the sonnet 'No worst, there is none'

   Those who have not suffered may indeed not take others' sufferings seriously. The writer of the Letter to the Hebrews makes the point that in Jesus we have a high priest who has entered into the depth of human experience. 'We do not have a high priest who is unable to sympathize with our weaknesses, but we have one who in every respect has been tested as we are' (see Hebrews 14:15). Though we would not wish serious sickness or the painful results of accidents or natural calamities upon anyone, those who have endured such experiences can be used to come alongside others in their times of trouble. Their awareness of what it feels like to suffer is invaluable; their knowledge is not just from theory, but learned in the school of human experience. In that way, we can see how God can use a time of sickness or adversity for our benefit and the benefit of others.

2. A lot of praise as it is expressed in the Bible, in the psalms or in the hymns and songs of the church, is based on thanksgiving for deliverance. As the hymn 'Praise my soul the King of heaven' puts it

   'Ransomed, healed, restored, forgiven
   Who like me his praise should sing?'

   If you compare all the words of this hymn, (Together in Song no. 134) including the verse 'Frail as summer's flower we flourish', which is missing in some hymnals, you will see that it is a paraphrase of Psalm 103. We can sing the hymn with joy and enthusiasm when we have had some experience of the mercy and help of God in our lives. It is a great hymn of praise for healing. Isaiah records King Hezekiah's prayer after his recovery from sickness (see Isaiah 38:9-20). Clearly he is a changed man and he can say 'It was for my welfare that I had great bitterness; but you have held back my life from the pit of destruction'. His prayer becomes a song of deliverance and this attitude towards things is now a part of the life of his spirit. When we have been in a dark place and come through it, it can become an unforgettable part of our experience, a rich but deep vein of gold within us.

3. A time when we are laid aside by sickness can be a time of reassessment in our lives, a time for seeing things we had not noticed before. The writer can recall a number of pastoral conversations of some depth with people who were forcibly removed from their hectic lifestyle or their high-pressure job by sickness or injury. We can learn

that we are not indispensable at work or at home – others can get on without us. In long periods of being alone and enforced rest, we can realize in a new way the things that are of greatest importance to us, and what is of lesser importance. At times when our very life is threatened we may turn to God in our need and be changed in remarkable ways. Important decisions about our relationships and responsibilities can be made in this environment when we are faced with the possible loss of all that we have built our lives upon. Sickness is also a time to develop a new sense of stewardship about our health, our diet, our life style, and our family life. Why then should we pray for healing if the sickness is of benefit to us? Surely it is better to be well than to be sick – who does not desire a return to health? Indeed we may ask for another period of our life to have opportunity to do things differently. God does not want us to go on being down in the pit forever. He wants us to live again and to praise him. The sickness time might be beneficial to us, but so would a time of health. Well might we pray 'Lord restore me that I might give thanks to you' or in the words of the psalmist 'I will tell of your name to my brothers and sisters; in the midst of the congregation I will praise you' (Psalm 22:22). There should be a place in our worship, not only to pray for the sick and suffering, but also for people to tell of mercies received and healing experienced.

4. There is sometimes benefit in healing being a gradual process rather than happening suddenly. Deep healing from within may be much better than quick external repair. A time of restoration is needed after many illnesses and injuries, a time for rehabilitation and rebuilding. A person who has had serious sickness, or shock and trauma through what has happened to them quite suddenly, needs time to be made whole again. So an important part of healing work is in the after-care and the time which we give ourselves for recovery. This should be a subject of prayer just as much as the request for healing.

There are ministries of sensitive pastoral care and gentle encouragement needed for those in recovery. Too much haste and impatience for quick healing may be detrimental and only put too much pressure on the patient who is shaky after serious sickness or injury. In the faith community we need wisdom in caring for the sick and ministering to them and the way we approach our own sicknesses. May God help us to make good use of our times of sickness and our times of recovery. May we not be afraid to ask for healing, but realize that there may be wisdom and benefit in slow recovery when we are, perhaps, looking for rapid results.

For thought and discussion ....

1. In what circumstances have you or others you know experienced benefit from a time of sickness or being laid up by injury?
2. What kind of person do you seek out to be your helper or encourager in time of need?
3. Is there opportunity given in your church community for people to tell of their experiences of healing? How is this done or how might it be done?
4. Discuss together what is involved in the work of recovery and rehabilitation after serious sickness or accident. What role can the church community, chaplains or pastoral workers have in this area?

STUDY 16:

WHAT PART DOES MEDITATION PLAY IN HEALING?

Begin by reading ....

1. Psalm 62
2. Isaiah 30:15
3. Mark 6:30-32
4. Matthew 11:28-30

Some reflections ....

1. Meditation and its deeper counterpart, contemplation are forms of prayer which can help promote our wholeness in body, mind and spirit. We might be accustomed to vocal prayers - prayers spoken out loud with a form of words which make sense to others. Such prayers may be the prayer of a person leading in ministry or worship or part of a formal liturgy. They may be prayers said or sung together like the Lord's Prayer or the Gloria in Excelsis (Glory to God in the highest ...) They may be prayers uttered at a prayer gathering or at a meal table. What is called 'interior prayer' is also very important – talking or listening within ourselves to God. As we grow in the practice of prayer and worship we become more aware of the importance of interior prayer and having an inner attitude of prayer and worship. Perhaps this is what Paul meant when he exhorted us to 'pray continually' (1 Thessalonians 5:17). The psalms speak of being quiet in God's presence (Psalm 62:1), of being still and knowing God is present, and always there for us (Psalm 46:10). It is wise to begin all times of prayer with a process of quietening down, deliberately putting ourselves in a quiet and uninterrupted place and opening up our inner being to God. The psalms also include some interior self-talk: 'Find rest, O my soul, in God alone' (Psalm 62:5). In Psalm 27 the psalmist has a conversation with his heart and with God: 'My heart

says of you "Seek his face." Your face, Lord, do I seek.' (verse 8). In the gospels we see that Jesus withdrew for times of private prayer. He also encouraged his disciples to 'come apart and rest a while' with Mark adding the comment that many were coming and going and they had no leisure even to eat (see Mark 6:30-32). The familiar words of Psalm 23 remind us that the Lord, in caring for us, wants to lead us to quiet and refreshing places. 'He leads me beside still waters; he restores my soul' (Psalm 23:2,3).

2. What is the difference between meditation and contemplation? Meditation usually refers to thinking over things in our mind, taking, perhaps, a biblical text or phrase and ruminating upon it. It may involve using our imagination – picturing ourselves as present at one of the gospel happenings, listening, observing, being part of the crowd. In meditation we can meet Jesus, say words to him and listen to what he says to us. Contemplation refers to a deep level of prayer. The activity of the mind ceases and we go into a deep place of being at the level of the spirit. We rest in the embrace of God's love: 'My beloved is mine and I am his' (Song of Songs 2:16). Most of us need some practice to be able to remain in a state of contemplation for a time. We are so used to a busy, active life with plenty of distractions; we keep wanting to jump up and do things; we live in a world where everyone seems to be short of time. Even when we go to church to worship, it can be very active and busy. We need to seek out a time and place for quiet meditation and reflection and then let ourselves slip into that deeper mode of contemplation.

3. When we are sick or injured the focus is very much on the body and what is happening to it. We cannot help that, as our body is crying out to us, clamouring for attention. Yet our mind and spirit are important resources for us. Healing can come to the body through the mind and the spirit, for body, mind and spirit are closely interconnected. If we

practise some meditation or contemplation we may find beneficial results for our bodies. We can picture God's healing light flowing into every part of our being; we can focus that laser of healing light upon a damaged or needy part. Perhaps this may be difficult to do if we are ill, but others can do it for us and with us. In our prayer of faith and meditation we can imagine this flow of warmth and light. To change the image, we may think of a flow of pure water from God, washing and cleansing a diseased or damaged part of our being. Jesus promised that he would supply his water of life for any who were thirsty or needed his refreshment. These are good images to work on and use and there are plenty more in the Scriptures and in a creative imagination.

4. Meditation is meant to be essentially simple, not complicated. The simpler the better. Take a rose and look at it – 'Lord, help me to unfold within'. Hold a seed in the palm of your hand – 'you have planted faith in my heart .... help it to grow'. Be observant of what is around you. God may be speaking to you through what you see or what you hear. Write down some questions you have of God and see what answer springs to your mind. Rejoice in your times of aloneness, and make sure you have some. It's good to see friends and visitors, but too many can be very tiring and put too much pressure on you if you are sick. Light a candle and let it go on burning to remind you of Jesus' continuous presence with you. 'I am the light of the world' he said 'whoever follows me will have the light of life' (see John 8:12). Do not be afraid: he is with you night and day and in the end will call you into his light.

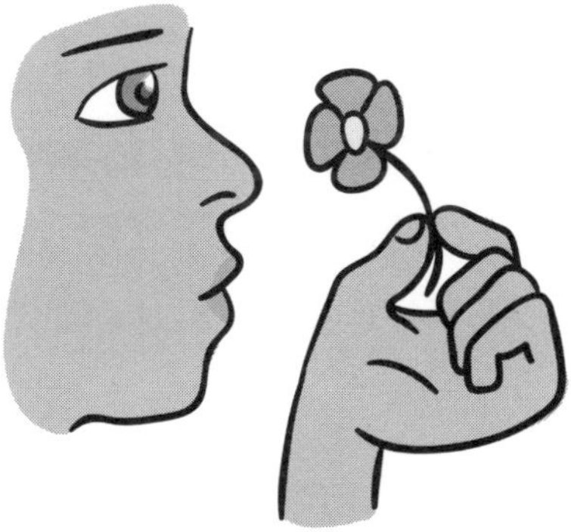

For thought and discussion ….

1. What have you learned of meditation or contemplation in your life? Share insights and experiences.
2. How might we help each other grow in the practice of meditation?
3. Think of the beneficial healing effects of meditation. A number are discussed in the above reflections, but you may have others to suggest.
4. Have a time of silence focussing on the presence of the risen Jesus in your midst. After the time of quiet you might share with others what you heard and saw.

STUDY 17:

HOW DO WE PRAY WITH AND FOR THOSE WITH CHRONIC DISABILITIES? IS IT GOD'S WILL THAT THEY ARE LIKE THAT?

Begin by reading ….

1. 2 Samuel 9
2. Job 7:1-11
3. Wisdom 11:23-12:1 (from The Apocrypha)
4. Acts 14:8-18

Some reflections ….

1. The name Mephibosheth is a tongue twister for those who have to read the Bible in church if 2 Samuel 9 is chosen as a reading! Mephibosheth, the son of Jonathan and grandson of Saul, was crippled in both his feet. In King David's presence he referred to himself very disparagingly – 'What is your servant, that you should look upon a dead dog such as I?' David, however was determined to show kindness to Mephibosheth for Jonathan's sake, and arranged for him to eat at David's table and be treated as one of his sons. There has been a special care shown in the Judaeo-Christian tradition for those with disabilities and the challenge is always there to provide for their needs without being in any way patronizing. In our times there has been increasing recognition of the problems and difficulties facing disabled people and we can be thankful for this. We struggle for words to describe such people, not wishing to disparage them or their abilities, or to make them feel marginalized. We need to honour their dignity as human beings and recognize their gifts and talents. One would hope that the Christian community would have a special sensitivity towards them, without any whiff of condescension.

2. One of our constant tasks is to break any connection in people's minds between misfortune and sin. In some societies disabled or disfigured people have been shunned on the assumption that they or their parents must have sinned. Jesus encountered this attitude when he was confronted by a man who had been blind from birth. When asked who had sinned, Jesus gave a very definite negative answer. He spoke of the man's blindness as giving opportunity for God's works to be revealed through him (see John 9:1-3). Many disabled people have not been cured of their disablement, but some have been able to turn their physical impairment to good effect. The life and achievements of Helen Keller spring to mind. Though blind and deaf in infancy she learned to speak and write; she wrote several books and helped wonderfully in the education and encouragement of those visually or aurally impaired. To feel that a physical or mental condition is the result of sin and to wear that condemnation would be very destructive and damaging.

   We need to be released from such negativity in our attitude to ourselves or others. The Book of Job reminds us that human calamity and suffering are not a punishment for sin, though Job's friends, in their traditional religious attitudes, thought so. However the book gives a place to the prayer of complaint; Job complained in the bitterness of his soul, and that is quite understandable. Our God is big enough to hear such a prayer and can help us to move on from that state of anguish and bitterness in due course. Better times do come for Job who in the end has a great period of restoration and blessing in his life. It may not be so for someone facing permanent disability, but they may have moved with faith and courage past the point of bitterness to a place where some positive steps can be taken to find ways of living fruitfully.

3. The statement in Wisdom 11:24 that God loves all things that exist, and detests none of the things that God has made, is basic to faith. Even if others might avert their

eyes from us or not know how to deal with us, we believe God looks upon us with love. The knowledge of that love and the love and respect for self which it engenders, enables us to be positive about ourselves and to be alert to possibilities for improvement. Someone has said that faith is possibility thinking. Faith saves us from ultimate despair. Faith and hope, the gifts of God's Spirit, undergird and call us on. It is part of God's very nature, Paul tells us, to cause light to shine in darkness, and God is able to shine in our hearts with the light of faith and hope. That light shone in the life and ministry and in the very face of Jesus Christ. It can shine in us no matter how dark our situation might seem to be (see 2 Corinthians 4:6).

4. When we pray publicly with and for people we should be very aware of the implications of what we say. 'Let your love be genuine' says Paul (Romans 12:9) and genuine love needs to shine through any prayer. Long, wordy prayers are best avoided, as we may start straying into explanations or solutions. It is best to pray according to need and by agreement with the person being prayed for, if they can express themselves. By faith we can step ahead of the person's present situation with them, praying for improvement and relief for them, for grace and courage in dealing with their life, and for the right help to come their way. To claim too much in the way of dramatic healing may put a heavy burden on them and on the believing community – 'if only we had enough faith ....' That is a dangerous path to follow. Healing is often a step by step process – a growth towards wholeness, and wholeness in mind and spirit is just as important as physical healing. The incarnation of Jesus, the one who is 'God with us', reminds us strongly that prayer needs to express Christ's coming alongside the person and his knowing what is happening to them in their life and being. Our prayer should express that faith.

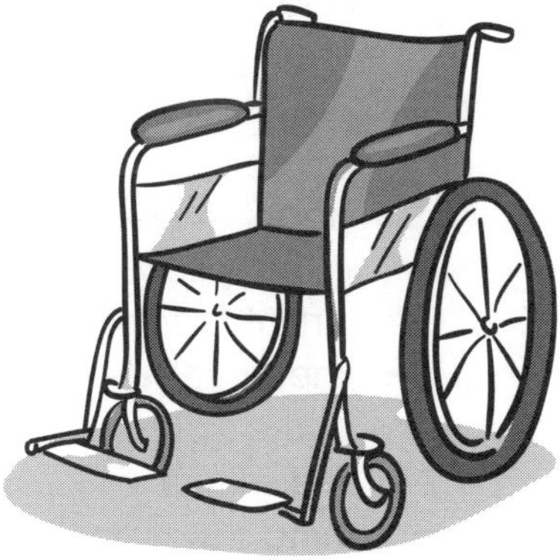

For thought and discussion ....

1. Think of (and share?) situations where work with disabled people has brought blessing and growth for you and for them.
2. Summarize together healthy and unhealthy attitudes towards disabled people. How do you think your church community handles this issue?
3. Find out about facilities or programs of care for disabled people in your local community. How can your church community relate to and support this work?
4. 'There is no fear in love' (1 John 4:18). Discuss this statement with respect to the way we approach people with impairment and disablement.

STUDY 18:

SHOULD WE HAVE SEPARATE HEALING SERVICES? WOULDN'T IT BE BETTER FOR HEALING TO BE INTEGRATED INTO THE REGULAR WORSHIP PATTERN?

Begin by reading ….

1. James 5:13-16
2. Mark 8:22-26
3. Acts 4:23-31
4. 1 Peter 4:7-11

Some reflections ….

1. It is clear that ministry of healing was not only a key part of Jesus' ministry, but as the church community was formed here and there throughout the Mediterranean world, 'signs and wonders' were not only expected, but actually happened as the gospel was proclaimed. The ministry of healing and the exercise of other gifts of the Spirit were unquestionably part of the church's life. Luke, in the Acts of the Apostles, describes the sense of awe that people had as they met and prayed together. Both Peter and Paul wrote of the importance of putting into practice the gifts that God gave to the believing community, but in such a way as all worked together for the common good and in such a way that God might be glorified in all that they did. It is likely that healing ministry was always part of what the gathered church did, and had a public character about it. 'The Lord worked with them and confirmed the word with the signs that accompanied it' is the way an early church ending to St Mark's Gospel puts it. (Mark 16:20) There is

gain in having public healing ministry as part of the worship pattern of the church community. People see the ministry and are reminded constantly that this is something which the church does and can do.

2. If we take Jesus' ministry as a model for us, we can see that sometimes he took people aside from the crowd to do healing ministry with them. There is a place for concentrated private ministry, and it is not always appropriate for the interference of prying eyes or the curiosity of onlookers who may be only looking for something sensational. We read that on one occasion Jesus drove out the crowd of onlookers and only took with him his close friends and disciples, Peter, James and John, and the close relatives as he ministered healing (see Luke 8:51-56). It is also clear from many references in the gospels that Jesus wanted to keep a relatively low profile to the ministry of healing so that it did not take over entirely. He ministered to people's need along the way, and as their needs were brought before him, but he sometimes hid himself away from the crowds and told people not to gossip about what they had seen and experienced. Perhaps he was concerned that his ministry of teaching and proclamation might be crowded out or pushed aside. A church which only concentrates on the meeting of human need, and has no program of teaching or building up disciples, may have the balance of its whole life disturbed. If people are always seeking the spectacular they may not deal with the ordinary and demanding tasks of daily living, serving and growing. Healing ministry, then, needs to be part of the church's life and worship, without taking it over.

3. Separate healing services are held by some churches to enable a particular focus in the services on needs for healing in body, mind or spirit. This separateness allows time for individual needs to be met; time can be given to this ministry where the Sunday morning's worship program may not easily allow this. Just as Jesus took his close

friends with him to minister to others, it is often helpful to gather a group of believers together so that the persons being ministered to are surrounded by those who can exercise the prayer of faith together in an agreed way. In the Sunday assembly there may be a lack of this quality of agreed faith – there may even be active disagreement over the exercise of healing ministry and various gifts of the Spirit and a lack of unanimity. There may also be a level of curiosity which does not quite give sufficient protection and confidentiality to the persons being ministered to. There can be great spiritual strength and effectiveness in separate healing services, or at least a Sunday service from time to time devoted to healing themes and healing ministry

4. James exhorts those who are sick to call for the elders (that is, the ministers and leaders of the church) to pray the prayer of faith over them, anointing them with oil in the name of the Lord. This teaching suggests that it is good for the sick person to take the initiative in asking for the ministry, or at least have others ask for them. In Jesus' teaching, he put quite a strong emphasis on asking – 'ask and it will be given to you, seek and you will find, knock and the door will be opened to you' (Matthew 7:7). To ask for a specific healing is an act of faith in itself and to have others focus together on a particular request is to exercise faith in an agreed way, trusting the promises of God given to us by Jesus. There is an argument for giving a whole congregation the challenge to move in faith together – to exercise their 'faith muscles', as it were. There is also a place for separate healing gatherings where those with some experience in the exercise of faith and who know something of the gifts of the Holy Spirit and their application can be there to bless and to minister to the sick. The Order of St Luke the Physician, an international and interdenominational fellowship of Christians who feel called to make the ministry of healing a regular part of their Christian vocation, does encourage separate healing

services, so that members of various churches in an area can come together to minister in this way. To do this at a time separate from the regular worship of their local churches, enables this genuinely ecumenical ministry to take place.

For thought and discussion ....

1. What happens about healing ministry in your local church? How is it done? Find out what happens in other churches and discuss the various approaches.
2. What safeguards do you think should be in place to protect confidentiality and to limit any unwelcome curiosity in the church community?
3. How can we best exercise the prayer of faith as church communities?
4. Why do you think Jesus on many occasions told people not to tell others about their healing? Is there any kind of limit we should place on advertising possible healing miracles that may have taken place?

STUDY 19:

ARE GIFTS OF HEALING MANIFESTED IN CERTAIN PEOPLE, BUT NOT IN OTHERS?

Begin by reading ....

1. 1 Corinthians 12:27-31
2. Romans 12:3-8
3. 2 Kings 2:1-22
4. Luke 10:1-9

Some reflections ....

1. When we read St Paul's First Letter to the Corinthians the answer to our question seems abundantly clear. The gifts of the Holy Spirit, including the gift of healing, are distributed variously amongst people. The gifts are to be used, not for division, nor for personal gain or aggrandisement, but for the common good. Just as the different parts of the body need one another, so in the life of the church, which is the body of Christ, we need the various gifts and a variety of gifted people. Nor should we expect everyone to have the same gifts. Paul makes this very plain when he asks rhetorical questions: 'Are all apostles? Are all prophets? Are all teachers? Do all work miracles, do all possess gifts of healing? Do all speak in tongues? Do all interpret?' Clearly, the answer to these questions is 'no'. We should not expect all believers to manifest gifts of healing, just as we shouldn't expect all believers to speak in tongues. The heeding of this teaching would have saved a lot of angst for those who have worried, even felt condemned or that they were second-class Christians because they hadn't spoken in tongues nor had any wonderful healings happen through the laying on of their hands. We do our various ministries as we are led and given opportunity, we do them in collaboration with one another and we leave the results to God. It is not appropriate for us

to boast about having particular gifts, nor to exalt one leader or minister above another on the basis of spectacular gifts. The gifts are God's and we exercise them so that God may be glorified, not ourselves. Paul speaks of 'striving for the greater gifts' (1 Corinthians 12:31) suggesting that we all should be open to developing gifts of the Spirit in our lives and ministries, and that some gifts are more important than others. As you will notice, he goes on in the same breath to talk of the importance of love and exercising all gifts in the church with love – the most important gift of all.

2. The Bible speaks in many places of particularly gifted people being sent by God to meet the needs of their time and generation. They were like burning and shining lights in a dark place. Jesus spoke this way of John the Baptist (John 5:35). God uses spiritually gifted individuals.

   Thus it will be with the 'gifts of healings' (the original Greek of 1 Corinthians 12:9 and 28 has a double plural). Some are specially gifted in this area. We might think of Agnes Sandford, Kathryn Kuhlman or Canon Jim Glennon. But in the light of biblical teaching we do not call such people 'healers', as we always remember that God is the source of all healing. It is also the experience of those engaged in the healing ministry that any member of Christ's body can be used as a channel of God's healing at any time, and according to a situation of need. God's gifts are there to be exercised by the community of faith and sometimes we step into the breach and minister in faith, though we might not have been accustomed to do so, or to see ourselves as gifted in that area. Paul's teaching about the exercise of gifts in Romans 12:3-8, suggests that we should minister, generally speaking, in our area of giftedness, but this teaching, sometimes referred to as 'motivational gifts' should not be applied too strictly. There are occasions when we move, and should move, into a new area of ministry. How else can we, or the church, discover gifts unless we are adventurous in this way? It would not be good to limit ourselves to only the gifts already experienced in the past.

3. When the church community gathers for worship, or to minister to a need that has been brought before it, or to plan some apostolic action together, we should believe that the gifts that are needed will be supplied by God. Either the gifts are already there, waiting to be exercised, but perhaps not yet discovered or realized, or we ask in faith that God will send to our church community someone gifted in the appropriate area. The underlying faith would be that if God calls us to do something, he will also equip us with the gifts and the gifted persons to do it. The church community, though, needs the kind of leadership which exercises the discernment of gifts and a spirit of encouragement running through its life, so that those who do start to exercise the gifts of God's Spirit on behalf of the community are sustained and supported. In his Letter to the Romans Paul makes special mention of the gift of encouragement (sometimes translated as the gift of 'exhortation'). Jesus, when promising the presence of the Holy Spirit to his disciples spoke of the 'counsellor', 'advocate', or 'helper' (see John 14:26). The word in the original Greek is 'paracletos' – someone whom we can call alongside us to help us. In other words, the Holy Spirit is an 'encourager' and the gift of encouragement is one of the signs of the presence of the Holy Spirit. Often a church member who may not be gifted in what could be thought of as the more 'spectacular' gifts, may exercise the gift of encouragement in a significant way. The gift is needed in the church community just as an engine needs oil. In fact, a healthy church community needs quite large doses of that important gift with leaders who know how to supply it and call it forth in others. When Paul speaks of some part of the body which seems to be insignificant having a significant role to play (see 1 Corinthians 12:22) he may have been thinking of that excellent gift of encouragement.

4. A bottleneck can occur in the church's life if there is a monopoly of ministry by one person or a small group of people. For sure we need good leadership in ministry, leadership itself being listed by Paul as one of the gifts of the Spirit (see Romans 12:8 and 1 Corinthians 12:28). However, there is

the kind of leadership that encourages the exercise of gifts by others, and a kind of leadership which stifles and is easily threatened. In the history of the church there has been a tendency towards clericalism – domination by ordained clergy who may have a vested interest in maintaining a monopoly, and not encouraging the ministry of the whole people of God. Where leadership is healthy, a deliberate attempt is made to identify and encourage gifts. This means that special care needs to be taken in using those with special gifts and who have solid experience in exercising a gift, and on the other hand recognizing that, when there is a need, God may use someone in a new way. Wisely, many churches run courses, or hold conferences on the recognition and development of gifts. We may note in our reading of Luke 10 that Jesus did not keep ministry to himself, but encouraged his disciples to step out into ministry in his name, and to report back and share their experiences of ministry (see Luke 10:17-21).

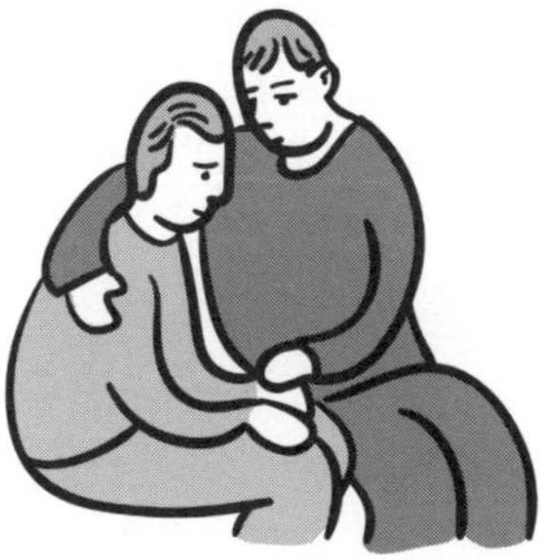

For thought and discussion ....

1. Having read the readings and reflections what is your answer to the question posed in this study?
2. What is your church community like in the recognition and encouragement of varying gifts of the Spirit?
3. Think about (and discuss?) the characteristics of good, and not so good, leadership.
4. Where have you seen the gift of encouragement at work or experienced the lack of it?

STUDY 20:

WHEN GOD KNOWS OUR NEEDS, WHY DO WE NEED TO ASK?

Begin by reading ....

1. Psalm 34:1-10
2. Isaiah 37:14-22, 28, 29, 36-38
3. 1 Kings 8:27-43
4. Luke 11:1-13

Some reflections ....

1. The whole tradition of our faith, and certainly as it is expressed in the Bible, is that God is responsive to prayer. Asking is OK. God hears us whenever we turn to him, at all times and in all places. It is not unusual when listening to the stories of those who have been in difficult and desperate places in their lives, and have cried out in their extremity to God, to hear how God has helped them. There has been an important turn around of events. When King Hezekiah was under extreme threat from Sennacherib, King of Assyria, he spread the letter he had received from Sennacherib before the altar of the Lord and prayed: 'Incline your ear, O Lord, and hear; open your eyes, O Lord, and see.' Hezekiah no doubt knew that the Lord knew what Sennacherib had written. In fact, later in the chapter the text has God saying of Sennacherib, 'I know your rising up and your sitting down, your going out and your coming in, and your raging against me' (verse 28). But it helped Hezekiah to make his prayer. In his human way he says to God 'Look at this, listen to this!' Prayer is like that. We do not doubt that God already knows, that God already looks upon us in our need. It is good for us, however, to express our prayer of request forcefully, even persistently; it is an acknowledgment of our need and our trust in God to be able to help us; it disposes us towards receiving what God has to give us and wants to give us.

2. Solomon's prayer at the time of the dedication of the temple in Jerusalem is a complete and moving one. He prays that

when all kinds of prayers and petitions and cries for mercy and forgiveness both from individual people and from the community as a whole are made in this consecrated place of prayer, that God will respond to the prayer. Even the prayer of the stranger and the alien is included. God's house is to be a house of prayer for all peoples. One can visit some of the great cathedrals of the world and not only wonder at the beauty and glory of the architecture, but sense that there is room for all kinds of people and their prayers and requests in such places. There are all sorts of secluded corners and chapels where private prayer can be offered. There is also the vast nave where a huge congregation can gather to pray in time of great need. There is room for all kinds of people and all kinds of needs and ways of speaking to God – truly inclusive places. Jesus spoke that way of his Father's house – heaven. 'In my Father's house are many rooms' (John 14:2). Our churches and church communities should be like that – inclusive and open to all kinds of need; places and communities where people are encouraged to address God in their need and to ask for human help and support as well.

3. Jesus often stressed in his teaching the importance of asking. He acknowledged that God already knows our need, but he encouraged us to ask; 'ask and you will receive, so that your joy may be complete' (John 16:24). In the Lord's Prayer he certainly encouraged us to ask – for God's kingdom to come, for daily needs, for forgiveness and deliverance from trials and tribulations. We hear that he did some asking himself. In one of his final prayers (recorded in John 17) he prays with and for his disciples and for those in the future who are going to believe in him through their word. 'Holy Father, protect them in your name that you have given me, so that they may be one, as we are one.' (John 17:11) In the garden of Gethsemane, Jesus asked the Father to take the cup of suffering away from him. The suffering was not removed from him, but he was strengthened to bear it.

4. There is definitely a place for asking. We may not understand what is happening to us, or why it is happening. We may be confused and bewildered, but we can always ask for help. That asking encourages our dependence on God our creator and redeemer, the one who is 'more ready to hear than we to pray'

(words from a collect in the Book of Common Prayer). Jesus' teaching following his giving of the Lord's Prayer, according to Luke's Gospel, bases prayer on our trust in God to give us things for our good rather than our harm. We think out good gifts and presents to give to our children, says Jesus, and we respond to their genuine requests. How much more God will give good gifts to his children. However, God gives a definite place for asking, and trusting his wisdom and ability to provide what we need most. It sometimes takes a long-term, retrospective view to see what God has given or withheld for our good. Overall, however, we come to know that we can trust that God is responsive to our need and our prayer. 'Cast all your care upon him, for he cares for you' (1 Peter 5:7).

For thought and discussion ....

1. 'Asking is OK.' Have you encountered those (perhaps yourself?) who have hesitated to ask? Why would that be? What growth may be required in us to help us do some asking?
2. As you look at the Lord's Prayer as recorded by Luke (Luke11:2-4), what strikes you? Share your thoughts about the prayer and the way we use it.
3. Sometimes you may encounter a situation where you or another person feels that they have been given a snake instead of a fish (see Luke 11:11). How do we deal with this?
4. Think of (and share?) times when you have realized that God is responsive to our prayers.